Darkness to Dawn

A Widowhood Survival Kit

Darkness to Dawn

A Widowhood Survival Kit

By

Diane Bullock

ISBN NUMBER: 1-58721-150-5

1st Books—Rev. 4/6/00

About the Book

This book was written specifically for the newly widowed. People in their first or rookie year of widowhood. It is during this period of time that people who are grieving feel the most frightened and alone. The author tells them that they are not alone, and that they will indeed come through this experience stronger and more in control of their fates and their lives.

The experience will be life changing, but the changes can be positive and can have a positive impact on the rest of the widow's life.

For instance, chapter 17 discusses the adjustments that must be made from being one of two to being alone, and the way the newly widowed are perceived by others. The question that is plaintively asked, "Hey, where did everyone go?" is answered as well as offering suggestions for ways to cope with the single status.

The author was widowed when she was 43 years old and has worked since that time with the Public Safety Department in a retirement community. She has experienced first hand the many problems that affect the newly widowed. Many of those experiences are in the book along with the way they were resolved.

Although it seems odd, some of the stories are pretty funny as reflected by the lady who had been widowed twice. She was a lovely woman in her 80's with blue eyes that twinkled and a serene smile. She was asked how she had dealt with being widowed twice. Her reply? "One day at a time, honey." Then she was asked if she would ever marry again. She cocked her head, grinned and replied, "No, from now on I'll just sleep with em!"

The whole message of the book is simple. There is life after the death of your spouse. You are strong, you are in control and you are not alone.

Dedicated to the memory of

ANTHONY LAIRD BULLOCK

May 26,1941 - November 29, 1986

Table of Contents

Forward

Okay, okay. The very worst has happened. In your wildest dreams you never thought that you would be alone. Your spouse has died and you must face the rest of your life without your partner. What could possibly be worse? How will you rebuild your life? What should you expect in the weeks and months to come? How can you prepare yourself for the challenges ahead? Are you smart enough, tough enough and strong enough? Will you survive this transition period with all your marbles? Of course you will!

I'm going to write a letter to you and put it in book form. I'll share my experiences with you and also share the experiences of people that I have met through my job as a public safety officer with a private security force.

Most of the people that I have met and talked with live in Pleasant Valley, a retirement city of about 10,000 people aged 55 and up. The last figure I heard was that the average age in Pleasant Valley is 78. Pretty impressive huh? A staggering number of our residents are widows and widowers. Not a great surprise when you consider the age group. Pleasant Valley is in the center of a large city in California. It is completely gated and the people who live there are very security conscious. I got a lot of my information about how people react to this traumatic experience from them and through their collective wisdom, formed many of my opinions about the grieving process.

I can almost hear you asking, "How the heck does she know what I'm feeling or how the heck can she be an authority?" The answer is that I am not an authority. I don't have a doctorate or even a degree in psychology. I do have a degree in life and more importantly, I care about what people are feeling at this time in their lives. Those are my credentials.

I met my husband, Tony Bullock, when I was 19 and he was 21. I thought he was the most handsome, charming and witty boy I had ever met. I had come to California for a little R and R after my grandmother's death. My grandparents had raised me and my grandmother's death was devastating to me. After I had been in California for about a month I met Tony. Tony could make me laugh by just cocking his eyebrow. On our first date, he took me to a pizza parlor where he did an imitation of Mitch Miller leading the band singing, "Be kind to your web footed friends for a frog may be somebody's mother." He sang all the verses and the chorus over several times. We laughed and laughed. I was hooked almost immediately. Luckily for me, he thought I was pretty terrific too. We had dated for almost a year when he finally got around to proposing to me. I thought I must be the luckiest girl in the world.

Reality soon reared its ugly head in the form of bills, dirty dishes, laundry and - a year after our marriage - diapers. Lots and lots of diapers. Tammy Marie Bullock was a never-ending source of wonder to me. She was followed 5 years later by Anthony Burlingame Bullock. Yes, I really gave a helpless baby the middle name of Burlingame. Tony and I raised our children on his income alone. He worked as a parts man for Mercedes Benz. It gave me a real understanding of what it means to be poor. I don't think we knew we were poor, we just knew we didn't have any money. We laughed, loved, cried, worried and did the very best we could with our little family. God must protect the ignorant because, although we didn't know what we were doing a good part of the time, we raised the most fantastic children.

Tammy has been married to a wonderful fellow named Mark for ten years and they have two lovely daughters. Tammy is a wife and mother, and has a second career as a computer systems engineer.

Anthony received his Ph.D. in physics from the University of California and is working on his post doctorate at a laboratory near here. I am happy to report that they both still love to spend time with old mom.

Tony had a congenital heart condition and had undergone open-heart surgery when he was 20 years old. I was aware of the problem and knew that in later years the problem could reoccur. However, I never thought anything bad could happen. Ah, the optimism of youth. It happens to everyone else, but never to you. Tony had regular checkups with a heart specialist and was always given a clean bill of health. As a matter of fact, the week before he died he had a complete physical and was told that everything was fine. Later, after his death, the doctors looked again at his test results and saw what could be thought of as future problems, but they were as surprised as they could be when Tony died.

Tony, the kids and I were watching a movie on TV. It was a cold, winter night, two days after Thanksgiving. We had a fire in the fireplace and had just finished dinner. It was an unremarkable night in every way. Tony was sitting next to me. He made a funny sound and died. Just like that. Tony was 45 years old when he died. I couldn't believe it. Shouldn't the angels have cried? The rest of that night is a partial blur to me. There was a tremendous cacophony of noise and people rushing around. As soon as I realized what had happened I started CPR on Tony, but was too late.

After the professional rescue people arrived, I started trying to make deals with God. I even promised to quit smoking if Tony could only live. I would try to be kinder to anyone that I met. I would start doing volunteer work. I promised to do anything and everything. No dice. There is a story in the Bible about wicked King Nebuchadnezzar. He had been warned time and again about his evil ways. Finally, God wrote in a finger of fire on the wall of his palace. Nothing the king did or said could change what had been written. It seemed to me that the finger of fire had written that Tony had died and nothing could change it. But I'm here to tell you all the little tricks I learned during my "rookie year" to help you through it.

I rode in the ambulance with Tony. He was already gone, but the kindhearted paramedic driving the ambulance put on a pretty good show for me. Lights and siren. The whole works. I kept looking into the back of the ambulance where Tony was lying. I remember thinking how much he would be enjoying the ride if he were aware of the lights and siren. I cannot remember ever being so cold. It seemed as though the cold went right through to my bones. It felt like a nightmare from which I couldn't wake.

When we got to the hospital the paramedics took Tony inside and put him on a table. No one worked on him and they all left the room. I think at that moment I finally began to understand that Tony really had gone to God. I felt as though I would shatter into a million pieces and I remember telling myself over and over that I would not lose my mind.

A nurse entered the room and took me to a private room for families. I sank to the floor and stayed there for the next hour or so. I was afraid to get up. I don't know why. Shock I suppose.

My father-in-law arrived and went in to say goodbye to his only son. After Dad said his good by, we all got into the car and went home leaving Tony behind. It broke my heart.

We got home and the ceiling fan was still running over the chair where Tony had died. It seemed so strange to me that things were just as they had been and yet nothing would ever be the same again. The tremendous challenge of surviving the tragedy and helping my children survive had begun.

Chapter 1

WHY? WHY? WHY?

The time immediately following a loved one's death is a time of complete shock and disbelief. Even if you have been expecting this awful thing to happen, it is still a shock. Many emotions are present during this time. Grief will come later. The first feeling that I remember is fear. Awful, paralyzing fear. Fear of everything and yet fear of nothing. I have always had a phobia about bees. A couple of days after Tony's death, I was sitting up on the hill overlooking the San Francisco Bay. I was thinking about all the sea captains' wives watching the bay and waiting for their husbands to come home. I was imagining how it must have been for them. A yellowjacket landed next to my foot. In normal times I would have let out a yell and taken off running. It has always been the greatest source of mirth to my family and friends. Some of them even imitate my yell and run technique. Not this time. I just looked at the bee and said, "Go ahead, take your best shot". I knew nothing could hurt as much as what I was feeling then. That feeling passes pretty quickly. I'm just as scared of bees now as I always have been, and behave like a perfect idiot if one flies too close to me. My windmill technique for escaping bees still provokes laughter everywhere.

At work I met a woman whom I will call Grace. She called 911 after her husband collapsed and died. She and her husband had been married for 50 years. He was not ill and his death was a terrible shock to her. I remember her saying over and over, "Billy, you must get up now." Her shock was deep, and as I held her hand and told her that he was gone, I could tell that although she heard me, she didn't really see me.

I taught her a technique that I call "time out." When the emotions become too painful to bear, in your mind you visualize a quarterback on the football field putting his hands together and signaling for a time out. For a second or two you think about anything that is pleasant to you - a grandchild's smile at Christmas, the ocean rushing to meet the shore, the sunrise over the mountains, or anything else that you enjoy. Your mind is an amazing tool, and giving it a quick break helps tremendously. This technique can be used over and over again in the weeks and months to follow. Grace told me many months later that she had used this exercise many times and it had worked for her. I saw her not too long ago, she is doing well and was dashing off to a table tennis tournament.

One woman who I will call Mabel suffered from Alzheimer's Disease. Mabel was somewhere in her 80s. Her husband of many years had died and her terrible fear and grief were heartbreaking. She could not understand what had happened or why he wouldn't answer when she called him. I sat with her in a room adjoining the room where the paramedics and rescue personnel were working on her husband. Although she had great difficulty understanding the here and now, she remembered her love of gardening. She was amazing and we talked for over an hour about different flowers and plants that she had grown over the years. The fear of what was happening in the next room would come over her and I would listen while she talked about her husband. After ten minutes or so I would put my hands together and she would follow suit. She would then go back in her mind to a happier time.

I was contacted by her family several months later and told that Mabel was in a controlled living situation with full-time care. According to her family she was doing very well and because of our talk that day, has a flourishing window garden. Wonderful!

One of the things that I have heard over and over again is the question "why?" There is no answer to that except "why not?" If we live long enough we all suffer losses. Remember that it is okay to question why this has happened. It's okay to be mad or sad or any other emotion you may feel. Don't beat yourself up over showing and feeling emotion.

A neighbor of mine approached me several months after Tony died and expressed her sympathy. I don't know what came over me, but in my best Sarah Berhardt imitation I replied, "Don't pity me, I've lived a love story," turned on my heel and flounced into my house. My toes curl in embarrassment when I think of that now, but at that time it was an honest expression of my grief. Embarrassing? You betcha!

Don't dwell on that stuff. People should understand. If they don't, tough. You'll probably say lots of goofy things during your rookie year. Don't worry about it. It is no big deal. Just move on and forget whatever you said. If you can, teach yourself to laugh over some of these things. It is difficult to laugh when your heart is broken, but try. The benefits from laughter are many. You will probably have to force yourself at first because there is nothing funny about what has happened. Pick out little things in everyday life that strike you as odd or unusual. When you have time, remember these things with humor.

I remember that at Tony's memorial service, a woman that I had known for many years was there dressed in a most unusual outfit - pink satin shirt, blue jeans and cowboy boots. Her husband was wearing a matching outfit. She was carrying a purse that looked like a panda. It was black and white with little paws hanging down. The top of the purse, where the zipper was, looked like the panda's back. The thought occurred to me that it would take a lot of training to get that panda to hold still long enough to put your hand into his back. Believe it or not, even though I was brokenhearted over Tony's death, I had to bite my lip to keep from laughing. I was so sorry that Tony wasn't there to see it. He would have been hysterical with laughter. Even writing this ten years later, I smile at the memory. Tony's death and memorial service were among the very worst moments of my life, but even at that awful time, something funny stays in my mind.

Your sleeping patterns will be changed for quite a while. Sometimes even for months. During the wee small hours you will have time for your thoughts. It's an excellent time for sorting through all your fears. I know it sounds crazy to be sitting in the dark while everyone one else in the world seems to be asleep, thinking about everything that has happened and maybe even laughing a little about some of the things that seemed strange or unusual, but you'll be amazed at how much this quiet time will help in the months to come.

The first couple of months after Tony died, I would awaken at 3 or 4 in the morning and be unable to get back to sleep. Tony had been a noisy sleeper, snoring, snorting and thrashing around. We had a Labrador retriever named Buddy. I coaxed her into sleeping on Tony's side of the bed. Buddy was an old dog and snored like mad. Buddy would chase rabbits in her sleep, snore and thrash about. Many times I would start to awaken, hear Buddy snoring, and be able to go back to sleep. Now, now, I'm not saying that a good dog can replace your partner. I'm only saying that there are many techniques that you can use that will help a little bit. Many little bits make a big deal.

Another trick that I learned was from a widow named Barbara, who told to take pillows and form a makeshift body under the covers on the other side of the bed. When you are half asleep it is comforting to feel that mound of pillows and to feel not quite so alone. I read that George Burns couldn't sleep after his Gracie died, so, he moved over to her bed. He wrote later about that being the turning point for him.

Turning your bedroom into a retreat helps too. Take your favorite books, pictures, music and paintings and redecorate the bedroom. Maybe you always liked a particular picture, but your spouse hated it. Well, now is the time to hang it on the wall. Music is helpful too. Bring a record player or tape player into the room and stock all your favorite music. It doesn't matter if it's opera or rock and roll, whatever you like will work just fine. Play your music, read any book you enjoy, or just retreat to your special, safe place and give yourself time to come to terms with what has happened. A little Elvis Presley and Neil Diamond at high volume helped me a lot. I'm sure it didn't find a great deal of favor with the neighbors. None of them ever complained, so guess it must have been okay.

Try to think of this period of time as your rookie year. It is a year of firsts. Your first Christmas,

Thanksgiving, anniversary, birthday and other special days, alone. Just as in other experiences in life, it will take effort on your part to adjust to and deal with the different challenges that each day will present. You can do it!

I have a good friend named Diane Steinberg. She and her husband, Jack, were married for 36 years when he died. Diane and Jack were the "fun couple." Everybody knows at least one. Diane is a lovely blond woman, so pretty that she had even done some modeling. I like her anyway. Jack was big and brusque. He was a warm and loving man. His kindness belied his "been there, done that" look. He and Diane raised three daughters. I can remember evenings at their home being filled with laughter. Both Diane and Jack had wild and wacky senses of humor.

I remember one incident in particular. Diane and I were invited to a Christmas party for the employees where we worked. It was going to be all women so Jack and Tony were not going. I have no idea where in the heck we got the idea, but we thought it would be really funny to show up in Santa Claus boxer shorts with color-coordinated blouses. We dressed slowly because we had to stop every few minutes to collapse in laughter. We looked ridiculous. Jack and Tony had very little to say about our unusual "look." Raised eyebrows were the order of the day.

When we arrived at Bobbie's (a co-worker) home for dinner, she threw open the door, took one horrified look and asked in a shocked voice, "Is it Halloween?" The rest of the guests were dressed in lovely outfits, and while welcoming us warmly, were obviously amazed by our look. The rest of the evening was spent with Diane and me convulsing into uncontrollable laughter. There is a picture of that evening floating around somewhere. One of the gals suggested blowing it up and putting it into the window of the store where we worked. Thankfully, no one acted on her suggestion!

Jack and Diane had retired to a mountain community in the Sierra foothills and we had been out of touch except for Christmas cards. She wrote to me about two weeks after Jack's funeral. In her letter she said, "Di, I need the tools to survive this. Please tell me how you got through Tony's death." She gave me the idea for this book. I wrote to her every week or so for the next year with the tips and experiences that I am sharing with you. I am delighted to tell you that Diane has come through her rookie year with flying colors and is well on her way. She has gotten a job to fill some of the hours and has reestablished a busy social life with her family and friends. She has even moved back to this area to be near her daughters.

Chapter 2

Holy smoke, I must be losing my mind!

The funeral is over. Most of the casseroles look even worse than when they first arrived. Who ever invented Jell-O molds anyway? Let's hunt them down and take our revenge! The cheeseballs are starting to grow things in the refrigerator that would make any mad scientist proud. People aren't coming as often as they did before. You can't remember who has called and notice that you have big holes in your memory.

Are you losing your mind? Not at all. It is perfectly normal. Everyone I have ever talked to has large holes in his or her memory regarding the first weeks or months after a traumatic experience. If you could see my memory on a screen, it would probably look like Swiss cheese. It is Mother Nature's way of protecting you from the most painful times. Some of the memories will come back. Others are gone. Probably no big loss, because it's a pretty yucky time, very stressful, and the mind - that wonderful tool - takes over and protects you from the worst of it.

This is the perfect time to baby yourself. Never mind all that "stiff upper lip" nonsense. Cry if you want, yell at the Fates, kick a tree. Do whatever you need to do to ease the stress. For a lot of people, the most helpful thing is to talk, talk, and then talk some more.

It was really easy to spot any friend of mine during that period. They had a glazed and dazed look in their eyes. I talked their ears off. Looking back, I'm amazed that my friends didn't run for the hills when they saw me coming. God bless them, most of them are still my friends.

I have a friend named Donna Wolverton. She is more like a sister to me than a friend. We have been friends for close to 30 years. We became friends when our children were little. She is the kind of friend we all need. I could tell her that I just murdered the Queen of England and Donna would try to justify my action. I would do the same for her. Friends like Donna are pure gold. We all have at least one. She was with me every day for several weeks after Tony died. I talked her ears off and then talked some more.

I don't remember a lot of what I said, but Donna reminded me the other day. She said, "You were totally goofy for the first month or so. You would ask for a stiff drink and you don't drink. You went on a cleaning frenzy and you've never given a hoot about housekeeping. It was as though everything was upside down in your mind." That about sums it up. Goofy behavior is the order of the day. You can expect to behave in a bizarre way for up to two years. Your mind needs to adjust to the shock. Happily, you won't remember much more than I do. Isn't the mind a wonderful thing?

It would be impossible to maintain the level of emotion that you are feeling now. You are like a volcano. You must release some of the pressure and ease the stress and talking is probably the best way to accomplish this purpose.

Other methods work well, too. Start taking a short walk every day. Build up to a half an hour a day. It will help you to sleep better and improve your health. One of the problems involved in grieving is the strain it puts on your health. Walking is something constructive that you can do for yourself. It helps tremendously to be in control of something, anything, and it will help you to sleep better and eat better, too.

Chapter 3

Suicide
(or)
"I don't want to live without my love"

The depression that follows the death of your spouse is perfectly normal. Everyone that I have ever talked to has gone through a period of time in which suicide seemed to be an answer. Some people actually do kill themselves because they feel that they can't stand the pain and have nothing left to live for. Bullfeathers. It may take work on your part, but there is always something worth living for. Those people who give up and do take their own lives never have a chance to see if they will feel better in the morning. For them, there is no morning.

As crazy as it sounds, during my "suicide period" I remember envying the widows in India who were thrown on the funeral pyres of their husbands. I thought that for them the pain would be over. Sure, but everything else is over too. As time went by I realized that a funeral pyre is not the way to go. I don't care much for the weather if it gets over 75 degrees, let alone a funeral pyre. That phase was just part of the "widow crazies."

I commute to Pleasant Valley every day and I drive past the dam. I remember thinking to myself that I should just drive the car over the hill and down into the dam. All the pain would be over. Unfortunately, everything else would be over too. There would be no chance to see if tomorrow was better. My children would then have another parent to grieve. Besides, the car was paid for. No, it just wasn't an option for me and it isn't an option for you either.

Understanding is probably the best defense during this period of depression. Understand that what you are feeling is perfectly normal and will pass in time. There are warning signs that your depression is too deep for you to cope with alone and that you need intervention in the form of professional help:

1. Disposing of your possessions.
2. Saying your good-bye to friends and family.
3. Double checking to make sure all your affairs are in order.
4. Being unable or unwilling to think about tomorrow or all the tomorrows to follow.
5. Being unable or unwilling to talk with your friends or family.
6. A complete and total disinterest in anything or anyone around you.
7. Radical changes in your personal grooming, eating and sleeping habits.

If several of the things in the list above apply to you, perhaps you need to speak to someone who is trained to assist at this time. A psychologist or psychiatrist will be able to listen to you and help you cope until you are strong enough to cope by yourself. There is no shame in accepting this help. Everyone has periods in his or her life when things are just simply overwhelming.

If this list seems to apply to you, put this book down and call for help. It doesn't matter if you call the suicide helpline, a psychiatrist, a psychologist, a clergyman, a priest or a rabbi. You must call someone. Do this for yourself and all those who love you. It may be the most important call you will ever make.

If you are still reading and feel that while one or two things on the list apply to you, that they are transient feelings and will pass, you are probably right.

During my rookie year, sundown was the time of day that gave me the most trouble. The sun would start to go down and my tears would start. Somehow I equated it with the death of the day. I felt I could stand all the sadness, but sundown defeated me. It passed in time with the help of lots of lights on in the house at that time of the day. I don't know why it worked, it just did. The electric company should send me a thank you note. I probably kept their books in the black for months. It was however, worth it.

It is an awful feeling, but thank God, doesn't last forever and you can control it. Long walks, prayer, talking to friends and family, retreating to your room to listen to your favorite music or cleaning something, all are methods for dealing with the depression. The most important thing is to remember who is in control. You are. Although the depression will wash over you like a wave on the beach from time to time, you are in control and can deal with it.

You can help yourself during this time by making sure that you are eating a well-balanced diet. Supplementing your diet with a good multi-vitamin couldn't hurt. Take a vitamin every morning with your morning tea or coffee. Make sure you eat a piece of toast with it so you don't upset your stomach.

If your appetite has deserted you at this time, make sure that you eat a little something every couple of hours. Whether it's fruit or toast or a soft boiled egg. Make sure that you keep your tummy functioning on a regular basis, and that will help you avoid some of the unpleasant side effects of a radical change in your diet. Remember, even a couple of bites of something are better than nothing.

Most of us have raised children and you remember what you did when one of the kids was sick. It is perfectly okay to treat yourself the same way. You're not sick in body, but sick at heart, and you need to baby yourself a little bit at this time. By taking care of yourself at this time in your life, you will benefit all those who love you and are concerned about you. It will ease their minds to see that you are in control and making decisions that will benefit you, and in the long run, them too.

Chapter 4

Dreams

Many people experience vivid dreams in the weeks and months following the death of a spouse. It is common to dream that your spouse is alive and the two of you are talking about whatever the health problem was that eventually claimed the life of your spouse. Maybe a doctor has arrived on the scene just in the nick of time in order to save the life of your loved one. Happiness reigns supreme and then when you awaken, the reality becomes clear to you. I used to feel as though Tony had died all over again.

I was troubled by these dreams, they were pretty tough for me. I would usually be awake the rest of the night dealing with the sadness and the pain. It seemed to me at the time that these dreams were torture. During daylight hours I could cope, after a fashion, with the awful reality. At night, my defenses were down and these dreams packed a tremendous wallop. It was tough for me to get up in the morning and function with any degree of normal behavior. I was tired and depressed.

I consulted with my doctor following an unusually prolific, dream-filled week. He told me that these dreams were very common for people who are grieving. He called them "wish fulfillment dreams." My subconscious was taking over and giving me a break from the sadness. Of course, I have a little quarrel with my subconscious regarding whether or not these dreams were helpful.

A friend of mine, Leonore Jacobs, told me that in the Jewish culture, the dead comfort the living through dreams. That was the most wonderful thought. The combination of folklore, religion and medical advice helped me tremendously. I came to terms with the dreams and understood what was causing them. Once I had a clear understanding about the dreams and what was behind them, they no longer troubled me. I could and did go right back to sleep.

One evening I went into my bedroom and laid down on the bed. It had been a particularly rough day and a throbbing headache was making things even worse. I started to doze off. I was in that twilight between being wide-awake and sleep. I heard a sound near the sliding glass door in the bedroom and then I heard Tony's voice. He said, "It's okay Diane, I'm right here." I jumped out of bed, ran to the door and looked everywhere to find out what could have made the sound. Of course there was nothing there, and the only sound was the wind in the trees outside.

I didn't tell anyone about that experience for years. The only reason I'm telling you now is because quite a few people have told me that they have experienced things just like that. Most of these people were embarrassed about it and convinced that they were losing their minds. It is probably another example of our subconscious minds trying to dilute the pain a bit. I don't pretend to have the answer, it's just another example of the things that widows and widowers feel and live through.

I do know that both the dreams and hearing the voice of your loved one or feeling his or her presence in a room are normal experiences and nothing to be concerned about. You are not losing your mind. Most of us have felt the same things.

I like Leonore's explanation the best. She told me, "When you are strong enough and don't need that comfort so much, it will stop." She was right.

Chapter 5

Lemons, lemonade, tunnels and roller coasters.

If you can visualize yourself on a roller coaster you will realize that when you hit the bottom, the roller coaster starts back up. Your emotions are like that during your rookie year. One day might be pretty good. The next, all the grief hits again and you hit the bottom. Just remember that you will go back up again. As time goes by, the highs will not be so high and the lows not so low. The early period that you are going through now incorporates the roller coaster with a tunnel. You know that there is light at the end of the tunnel. You just have to keep going. Each and every time that you survive a really bad day and exercise control, you will be that much stronger. Probably doesn't feel like it, but it really is true.

You probably feel that your life is swirling out of control. One of the positive things you can do for yourself is take your life back and you have already started doing this. You have created a retreat for yourself, you're walking every day, you're talking to friends and family and you are helping yourself. You are in control. Certainly there will be moments when the tears flow and you can't control them.

A produce section at my supermarket comes to mind. One day even the oranges and apples had a distinctly salty taste. By the wildest stretch of the imagination, you could not say that I cry in an attractive way with my red nose, snorting and snuffling. No resemblance between me and Camille.

In the movie she was reclining on a chaise lounge in a lovely negligee with one silver tear on her cheek. In the movie, her character was dying of consumption, or as we call it now, tuberculosis. She looked gorgeous through the whole movie even while she was crying. She didn't even get a red nose. No, not me.

Just keep in mind that this is all perfectly normal. You're not losing your mind and will not end up in a rubber room with finger paints. When you hit the bottom, the roller coaster starts back up. You are doing just fine.

There is an old expression, "When life hands you a lemon, make lemonade." It explains the approach you need to keep in mind when trying to make the most sense out of this whole situation. Taking control of your life and helping yourself.

Chapter 6

Anger

"Madder than a wet hen". "Madder than a one legged man in a kicking contest". You can make up your own sayings to cover this emotional time.

A lot of people describe being angry at the person who has died. They're mad because their partner left them here alone. One woman, who had just lost her husband, turned to me and said, "I never believed that Bob would leave me". At the risk of sounding like a broken record, it is perfectly normal to feel anger. I cannot remember being angry with Tony, but I got mad at just about everybody else.

Donna reminded me the other day that I *was* mad because Tony left. It must have been in the murky, icky first week or so, because I have no memory of it. My conscious anger was more like a laser. It bounced all over the place and at targets that make no sense at all.

I was especially enraged by the fact that Ted Bundy was alive. Yes, Ted Bundy. I never met the man but I was incensed that he was breathing air, eating food, sleeping in a bed and living when Tony was dead. Where is the justice in that? A psychopath was alive and my Tony was dead. I was furious. I would love to be able to tell you that all that anger evaporated when Bundy was executed, but it wouldn't be true. I just moved on to other targets.

I wish I could tell you that my anger was logical and just. I can't, but I would love it if I could. Mostly, my anger never made any sense at all. The only way it makes sense is if you look at the whole picture. A little like a pit bull in a room full of steak bones. I didn't know which one to bite first.

A woman that I met at a widow's group, (my one and only visit) was a professor's widow. She was lovely and very articulate. You could tell at a glance that she had been grieving for quite a while. She was very thin and seemed almost ethereal. She had long, dark hair and big eyes. If she hadn't been so painfully thin, she would have looked like a beauty queen. She was telling the group about a colleague of her husband's who had taken some work of her husband's and claimed it as his own. As I watched her, this delicate, lovely and gentle woman turned into a tiger. Her voice rose several decibels as she declared, "If he doesn't apologize and give my husband credit for the work, I will never speak to him again". There wasn't a doubt in my mind that she meant every word. I wouldn't have been surprised to read in the paper that she took a punch at this fellow.

The most important thing about this anger you're feeling is that you are in control. You can stop yourself from yelling at someone who has said something totally stupid to you. For instance, "I know just how you feel. I grieved when my little dog Tippy died." Yeah, right! Every time you are faced with something totally asinine like the above statement and you control your pain and anger, you will be that much stronger. If you are unable to stop yourself from saying something you regret later, just remember that there is always tomorrow. Don't worry about it too much. Rome wasn't built in a day and it will take time for you to build up your self control. Don't worry too much about it. Time helps you in dealing with clods and thoughtless people. Remember, you won't be actively grieving forever, but clods are clods forever.

There will be many challenges for you in the months ahead, and as long as you don't throw up your hands in despair, you will be fine. All of us who have survived this awful time have many of the same experiences. Keep trying and you will succeed. The roller coaster will start back up again. You will laugh again, love again and live again. Maybe not in the same way, but you will live a complete and rewarding life again.

Chapter 7

Tranquilizers - Sleeping Pills - Alcohol

During the first weeks, or for as long as a month or two, you may need help from your doctor in the form of tranquilizers, sleeping pills, and other medication to help you through the worst of it. Your doctor will be the best judge of what is right for you. My best advice is to be completely candid with your doctor about what you are feeling. Most people in this situation are embarrassed about the tears and lack of control. Don't be. It is normal, and an accurate representation of what you are feeling.

It is perfectly okay to take these prescribed medications for a (short) period of time. The operative word here is "short." Be aware that it would be easy to become dependent on these chemicals. That would be a big mistake, because in addition to the grieving process, you would also have to deal with a chemical dependency.

A friend of my husband's has a sister named Linda. Linda is the kind of gal who always lived life on the edge. First one in the pool and the last to leave. She had a problem with drinking when she was in her 20s. She married and she and her husband raised her child from a previous marriage and were very happy together. Linda had been in an auto accident when she was in her teens. She went through the windshield and had the scars to prove it. For years after the accident she would have different surgeries to try to repair the damage. I believe that alcohol numbed the pain and she became dependent on it.

She went through several treatment programs and would be off the sauce for a long period of time and then, blam, something would go wrong. Back to square one.

Linda's husband died of cancer after a long and valiant fight. Linda nursed him to the very end. She did not work outside the home and was able to devote herself full-time to her husband. She was - in my eyes, anyway - the perfect partner to her husband. She was there for him every step of the way and I believe that because of her, his last months were easier for him, although the toll on Linda was devastating.

After his death, Linda's doctor prescribed various antidepressants and sleeping pills. Linda took them for about 6 months, then managed through sheer will power to get off everything. During this period I would see her on occasion and have lunch with her every once in a while. She was having the devil's own time of it, and after another 6 months or so the doctor prescribed more medication for her. The last time I saw her she was very reclusive. She rarely leaves her home and is completely dependent on the pills. She was unable to take control of her life because the tranquilizers have left her without her most valuable tool, her mind. Her mind is too numb for her to realize what is happening. God help her. I think of her so often.

The lesson here is very simple. As difficult as this time is for you, it is necessary. Every day that you try and succeed, you will be that much stronger and that much more confident. It takes a long time because you are going through so many changes and you're learning so much about yourself and the world around you as it relates to you as a widow or widower. No matter how painful, you need to experience these things in order to make the necessary adjustments in your life.

My grandmother used to say, "You can't make steel without fire." Sometimes it feels as if the fire is too hot, and that is when you use the techniques you have learned. Using "time out" is excellent, or you can retreat to your room, or take a nice long walk.

Using artificial methods for relieving the pain is, at this time, a mistake. You can do this without medication or alcohol.

The only exception I can think of is if you have always had a glass of wine with your dinner - I see nothing wrong with continuing this practice. Do not allow it to become two or three or four glasses, however. That could be the start of a problem. The last thing you need right now is another problem.

Chapter 8

Memories - Enemy or Friend

Years ago I knew a woman by the name of Ethel Peterson. She had been a friend of my grandparents. Ethel and her husband had been married for 30 years or so when he died. This lady stayed in the same apartment and continued caring for their son who was retarded. She impressed me so much because she always talked of her husband in the present tense. She celebrated their wedding anniversary as though he was still there, just in the next room. She would say things like, " Walter and I have been married for 41 years today and I baked this pineapple upside-down cake because it's his favorite," or "I am tatting this new tablecloth in Walter's favorite pattern. He loves it when I make things for the house."

Ethel lived for another 20 years after her husband died. She never deviated from her course and talked of him as though he were right there up until the moment of her own death. I don't know what happens when we die, but I sure hope she has been re-united with her beloved Walter.

For myself and others that I know, the memories are almost unbearable at first. A photograph, the smell on a jacket, a certain song, a familiar place, or any number of other things can trigger the memories. Tears are never far behind. The roller coaster starts back down again and the grief and loss roll over you. Perfectly normal, my dears.

Avoid the things that cause you more pain during this period of time. You need more pain right now like a dog needs more fleas.

The woman I told you about at the memorial service who wore the jeans and carried the panda purse has never been widowed, but she has been divorced, several times. She would suffer the agonies of the damned after each divorce. She would play the same record over and over again, usually, a country-western crying song. She would retreat to her bed, pour a large drink, and play the crying record over and over and over. I know this because she would occasionally call me and ask me to come to see her. I am not making fun of her, because she was dealing with these situations in the only way she knew. Holy cow, talk about counter productive. The more she drank and cried, the worse the situation became. Her memories were her worst enemy because they were colored with regret.

I was never sure, but I think maybe she enjoyed these episodes. They purged her soul and before you knew it, she would be dating someone else. She was and is a beautiful woman. It saddens me to think what things might have been like for her if she had only used some of the techniques that I have outlined for you. She is an intelligent woman and could have done anything with her life if she had only faced her problems realistically.

Memories are a lot like a savings account. You don't have to check them every day to make sure they are still there. Your memories will always be there and while they cause pain at first, in time they become old friends. It is wonderful to visit these memories in your mind. A lovely place to visit, but you can't live there. As you know by now, you have work to do in rebuilding your life. You are doing well and have accomplished a lot in this short period of time. Remember, control is the key. Every day that passes you are exercising that control a tiny bit more. Good for you!

I have dinner with my children every week or so. We are all so busy with our lives that it is difficult to get all of us together at the same time. We're usually going in 27 different directions. However, when we do get together, the memories of their father are brought out and we talk and laugh as we remember him. We howl with laughter when we remember how Tony mixed up his metaphors. He would say things like, "A bird in the hand, uh … uh … uh… doesn't have both its oars in the water," or "The ladder doesn't reach all the way, um, to the water."

We talk about his referring to our son Anthony as "boy" until Anthony was 12 or so. Anthony says he thought his name was Boy for years. That always sets off gales of laughter. My memories are old friends and yours will be too, in time.

The memories are something that belong to you alone. You are the best judge of when or how often to remember them. If they cause you a great deal of pain, avoid them for a while, in time they will give you a great deal of pleasure.

Years ago there was a TV show called *Hee Haw*. It featured country comedy and they had a skit that they would do on a regular basis. A man would go to see his doctor. He would always wiggle his arm around and say, "Doctor, it hurts when I do this." The doctor would slap at him and say, "Then don't do that!" I used the same advice without the slap. If it caused pain I didn't do it.

I read somewhere that who you are shows on your face. People who have been mean and rotten look the part and kind, gentle people have kind and gentle faces. The same is probably true of memories. The most important thing is to try not to visit your memories with regret. Yes, the person you shared these memories with is gone, but you have been left a wonderful legacy - the memories. Enjoy them. You earned them, and they are yours and yours alone.

Chapter 9

Sex

Yes, you read the title of this chapter correctly. It is about sex. During the rookie year of grieving and adjusting to your life, one of the things that will probably bother you will be the changes in your body because you are no longer sexually active. Your body had to get used to your being sexually active during your marriage. If you are like most people, your sex life was probably an enjoyable but routine part of your life and suddenly, no more sex. Of course, your body will revolt.

One of the ways that your body shows its displeasure is in the form of erotic dreams. Many people have told me about awakening during an absolutely wonderful erotic dream and wondering what the heck was the matter with them. Nothing is the matter. It's perfectly natural.

The first time that I awakened during a sexy dream, I was sure that I was losing whatever was left of my mind. I remember thinking, "How in the hell can I be dreaming about things like this when Tony is dead? I must be going crazy. What kind of pervert am I?"

The very next day I went down to the library, and after looking around to make sure no one was watching me, I headed to the human sexuality section. I can remember thinking that I should be wearing a dirty raincoat like the "Fernwood Flasher" on the TV show "*Mary Hartman - Mary Hartman*". I skimmed through several books regarding human sexuality, all the while glancing around surreptitiously to make sure no one was observing me.

The problem with this situation is that the subject is so private. My advice would be to confide in a close friend. I told Donna some amazing things during that first year. She could probably blackmail me for the rest of my life if she wanted to do so. She wouldn't of course. That's why you should choose your confidant carefully. If you are not comfortable confiding in anyone, don't. If you do need to vent those feelings, do so. Remember the doctor on "*Hee Haw*". If it causes you pain or discomfort to discuss it, don't.

Again, the broken record. This is all perfectly normal and is to be expected. Most people don't talk about this subject, but it is a normal part of your life and if you need to talk about it do so, as you will probably continue to dream these dreams for an indefinite period of time. Talking will ease the anxiety that you feel. Most importantly, don't be embarrassed about this perfectly normal part of your life.

Believe it or not, I don't really have any advice for you except to visit your doctor and make sure that you are in good health. If there is no medical problem causing you difficulty, it is probably abstinence that is causing it.

I do not recommend that you have an affair or anything like that at this time in your life. You're not ready for a romance with anyone and you have many things to work through during this year without the complications of an emotional attachment that may or may not work out.

Think of yourself as a big cat in a big litter box. Don't do anything that you can't cover up later. All of us make mistakes during this period of time. Just make sure they are small mistakes that you can cover up or fix. I know of people who, in a very short period of time, find someone else and build their lives with this new person. I think they are the exception rather than the rule.

You have a lot of adjustments to make during this year and you need to be in control in order to make the necessary adjustments.

At some point in the future, you may be ready to meet someone, fall in love and make your life with that person. Right now you have too much work to do and really don't have the time to devote to a relationship. Besides, being in a relationship takes a lot of time and energy, time and energy that you don't have right now.

These statements are, of course, generalizations. There are exceptions to every rule and I know of people who remarry almost immediately and remain happily married.

My father-in-law comes to mind. He and my mother-in-law married when they graduated from college. It was a love match. They raised two children. Both were professional people and built a very nice life for themselves. My mother-in-law was one of those people you usually only read about in books. She was an accomplished pianist, horsewoman, needlepoint expert, raised show dogs, and held a very responsible job with a large bank. As a matter of fact, she was an executive with the bank in the days before it was socially acceptable for women to have careers outside the home. In addition to all this, she was a loving wife and mother.

In 1964, she was diagnosed with inoperable cancer. She died three months later. She faced her death with the same kind of courage that she had always shown toward life. She was a no-nonsense kind of gal. She had a wonderful sense of humor and even made fun of some of the symptoms of her disease.

The void left by her death in my father-in-law's life was horrendous. He was and is a very private man and didn't talk about it very much, but we could see the suffering on his face. He lost weight. His complexion was sort of gray, and although he was in his fifties when this happened, he aged before our eyes.

Approximately six months after Mother's death, he started looking better. We would have dinner with him and would remark later how much better he seemed to be. A couple of months later we were invited out to his home to meet the lady who was responsible for his improvement.

They were married after Mother had been gone for a year. The lady he married was, in our eyes, the complete opposite of Mother. She was a gal from the Midwest with a strong sense of family and values.

She was and is a perfect partner to my father-in-law. The love and care they show each other has been going strong now for over 30 years. We were delighted to see the bounce back in Dad's step and the twinkle in his eyes. Yes, for them it worked very well.

On the opposite side of the coin, I knew a man that I will call Ed. He and his wife were married for about 30 years when she died. He had a devil of a time adjusting and never really did adjust. His neighbors would talk about hearing him sobbing in the yard or the house. He met a lady who I will call Mary. They dated for a short period of time and married.

The marriage was an awful mistake. They didn't have anything in common except that they had both been widowed. She was a classic couch potato and he loved outdoor activities - fishing, hunting, camping, bike riding and every other form of exercise you can think of. She loved TV, reading, music on the stereo, and small dinner parties for friends. To say that they made each other unhappy would be an understatement. Whenever I was around them, the contempt between them made me cringe. They were civilized people and nothing insulting was ever said between them but their unhappiness was evident.

Ed and Mary stayed married until Ed's death. No two people could have been more unhappy. They were born and raised to believe that divorce was a sin and so they stayed married. I was struck by the lack of warmth in their marriage. They both went through the motions but alas, it was a terrible mistake for both of them.

I heard from Mary last Christmas, and she is happier than she has been in years. Ed has been gone for over two years now and she is involved in a relationship with someone who is much more compatible. As a matter of fact, she sounded almost giddy in her letter.

Ed and Mary could have saved themselves and others around them a lot of pain if they had only waited and gotten past the first year of widowhood before making such a big, life-changing decision.

Chapter 10

I couldn't have bounced a check, I still have checks left

Whether or not you have always paid the bills or handled different financial situations in your marriage, doing the bills and handling the investments will be a bit of a shock. Suddenly you are responsible for keeping yourself afloat financially.

Tony had always paid the bills. He loved it and would tell us that he put all the bills in a hat. He would pull them out of the hat once a month and pay them until the money was gone. Those left over had to wait until the next month. If they griped about not being paid, he threw them out of the hat.

I worked part-time and would turn my paychecks over to Tony, and he would give me an allowance. Money never mattered to me. Imagine my shock after his death when I had to learn how to pay bills. I have found that creditors are rather dull folks with no sense of humor.

As soon as you can think clearly you will need to take stock of your assets and liabilities. It will probably help if you do this at a certain time each month. If you start making your payments on a regular basis it will become second nature.

You may have insurance money or money that you held jointly with your spouse. Familiarize yourself with your financial situation and take it from there. You may want to consult with your lawyer. You may have to change jobs in order to make more money or liquidate some of your assets in order to make ends meet.

Be very careful making any decisions that you don't have to make during the first year because your judgment is probably screwed up. Remember that big cat in the litter box and let that be your guide.

You didn't learn to roller skate or ride a bike in one day and you won't learn how to run your financial life in one day either. It will take time and effort. Now, don't panic. You can do this. No matter what your political philosophy, now is a terrific time to be (conservative). Don't spend money you don't have to spend. Do you really need 7 pairs of designer jeans? Make sure that every dime that you spend is necessary to sustain your lifestyle. You may even have to cut back on your spending a bit. Although this will be challenging and a bit painful, after the pain you have lived through, it ain't nothing.

A lot of people feel smothered by the bills and the responsibility of owning a home. Be very careful making any changes in your lifestyle during your rookie year. It is best to just maintain your normal lifestyle.

I've known a lot of widows and widowers who have had a knee-jerk reaction to their homes and the memories associated with their homes. They feel that they have to get away and end up selling their homes during that first year, moving away, and after the dust has settled, wondering what in the heck they've done. By then it is usually too late to get back what they had and they have to absorb the loss. Big mistake. No matter how big the cat, you can't cover that one up! The best rule is to avoid making any big decisions until after the first year has passed.

As you already know, you cannot run away from this situation. The painful reality and the rebuilding of your life will follow you wherever you go. It is not healthy to try to run away. It is much better to stay where you are and make your adjustments from a position of strength. Political and military types love that kind of statement. They use it all the time, but in your situation it makes perfect sense. The decisions you are making and the learning process you are experiencing is much better faced from a safe and secure place - your home.

There are a lot of people in this world of ours who will take advantage of your vulnerability during this period of time. I know, I know, it's hard to believe that people could be so mercenary and so cruel, but it is a fact of life and you need to protect yourself from these scoundrels. It would probably be best during this period of time to limit your business dealings to people you know and trust. Your family lawyer can be invaluable to you in explaining your financial health.

It has been 10 years since Tony died and I know where every dime that I own is and I know what it is doing. It is sort of like having a problem child. You must keep track of this little creature. The same thing is true of your financial child.

In my work for the Public Safety Department, I have seen many examples of scams run by unscrupulous creeps who target the elderly. The one thread that runs through these scams is that the recipient will get something for nothing. The creeps target that little bit of greed that is in each of us. Without it, their scams would not work. The very best advice that I can give in this area is that if it seems too good to be true, it probably is.

If you remember that little saying, you probably will not be the victim of a scam. Do not let a single dime out of your sight unless you are darn sure where it is going and what purpose it is intended to fill. Don't worry about this financial stuff too much, just be aware and be wise. You didn't just fall off the turnip truck. You have a lot of knowledge about the world and the way it works as it relates to you. Use that knowledge and the good common sense that God gave you and you'll be just fine.

One case that I saw involved an elderly man, in his 80s. He had been contacted by one of these scam outfits and told that he had won a prize. He was instructed to send them some money to start the process. By the time Public Safety got involved he had already sent several thousand dollars to these creeps. The scam artists were so good at what they do that the victim was convinced that if he failed to keep sending money, he would lose out on the prize. By the time we intervened, he had sent them in excess of $15,000. He could not afford that kind of loss. It makes me livid that these creeps seem to get away with this kind of thing and there is a very low prosecution rate for them. They're pretty slippery. Again, the best advice is if it seems too good to be true, it probably is.

Chapter 11

Is there life after death

I wouldn't presume to get into a theological discussion about whether or not there is life after death for the person who has died. Frankly, I don't know. I sure hope so. Rather, this chapter will deal with your life after the death of your other half.

You have already made great strides toward rebuilding your life. You have made a safe retreat for yourself, you are walking every other day or so, you are taking care of the financial responsibilities in your life. Slowly but surely you are building a life for yourself. I'm not talking about the life you had before your spouse died, I'm talking about your life now.

I was talking on the phone to my brother, Bob, one day in the first 3-month period after Tony died. I can remember clearly wailing to him that I didn't know who I was. I had been a wife and mother for 25 years and suddenly, no Tony. Who the heck was I? My brother, God love him, is a no-nonsense kind of guy. He rumbled, "What are you, stupid or something? You're Diane. You've always been Diane and you will always be Diane, so cut the nonsense. Actually, he used a word other than nonsense, but you get the idea. Not terribly sympathetic, but it sure got the point across.

During this period of adjustment, remember some of the things that you enjoyed doing while you were married, things that you did without your spouse - horseback riding, painting, refinishing furniture, baking, cooking, playing the piano, or even bungee jumping. You can make your own list.

I met a woman named Lillie about 2 months after her husband died. She was reading a book outside her home. Actually, she wasn't reading as much as she was crying. I sat down beside her on the bench and she told me about her Sid. Lillie had lost most of her family during the Holocaust and suffered great tragedy in her life. She and Sid had raised 2 children on very little money. One of the things Lillie said to me stays in my mind. She said, "God can make any miracle, would it be too much to ask to have my Sid back?"

I got to know Lillie because she lives in Pleasant Valley and I would see her occasionally during the course of my duties with Public Safety.

She went through all the classic phases of grief. I would check on her whenever I had the time. I noticed that she was at home less and less as time went on and wondered what she was doing. Turned out that Lillie had turned her love for children into volunteer work for the Jewish Community Center and was working there with the children. She also works with Alzheimer's patients. Her wall was covered with crayon drawings that the children had made for her. She also went to work for several other charities and became busier and busier. She has been honored for her work by several charities and featured in the local newspaper. Good for Lillie. She sure turned a lemon into lemonade.

She still misses her Sid and will occasionally mention it to me, but she has built a life for herself. She is loved and respected by many and her life has meaning. She also has the most wonderful laugh, and I have had the pleasure of hearing her laugh - often.

At the opposite end of the financial spectrum is Catherine. I met Catherine when I was sent to take a report regarding an auto accident that she had been involved in. She had run her car into a tree. Her car was just barely moving when she hit the tree so there was not much damage. Catherine is a retired judge and an extremely accomplished woman. To say that I was impressed by this magnificent woman would be an understatement. During my association with Catherine I came to know her a bit and my admiration for her grew. Like Lillie, she also went through all the classic phases of grief.

Catherine got through her rookie year and started picking up the threads of her life again. She served on a presidential council, became involved again in the law, and spent a lot of time in Hawaii, where she had a second home. I know from having talked with her on several occasions that she still misses her husband, but she has gotten back into life. She is doing many things that she enjoys and is making a considerable contribution to the world around her.

Both Lillie and Catherine, even though they are so different they could have come from separate planets, took the same path after being widowed. They both became very involved and filled their time with what they considered to be worthwhile pursuits. The rest of us have benefited from their efforts, and they have rebuilt their lives. Bully for them! Lemons into lemonade.

Richard lost his wife after many years of marriage. He is a retired police lieutenant who lives in Pleasant Valley. He flew bombers during World War II. In my opinion, he is a true American hero. His interests are many and varied. He and his wife attended a lot of different functions. They were always "on the go", and they spent a lot of time with friends and their grown children.

Richard's wife became ill with cancer and for 3 years she fought the disease until it finally claimed her as its victim. Because the disease was so time-consuming and energy sapping for all concerned, Richard and his wife got into the habit of staying at home. After her death he was totally drained of energy. He went through all the phases of grief, starting with denial. His depression was the worst I have ever seen and didn't seem to get any better as time passed. I would hear from a mutual friend that Richard was seriously considering "eating his gun", a police euphemism for suicide.

Two people who know Richard asked if I would make a special point of dropping by his home and checking on him. I agreed and dropped in on him several times. I would also catch him outside when he was walking his dog. I would pull my security unit over to the side of the road and engage him in conversation every chance I got.

One day Richard looked at me and said, "Don't you have anything better to do than hassle honest citizens? Go find a crook or something." After that pronouncement, I must have looked shocked, because he threw back his head and howled with laughter. That seemed to be the new beginning for Richard, because he started getting out more, playing golf, attending the theater, having dinner out with friends, and he goes flying with a friend of mine. This hasn't happened all at once, but he does seem to be rebuilding his life. He still suffers from bouts of depression, but the degree of severity seems to be lessening. It has been 4 years since his wife died. I tell you about the time frame so that you will not feel that you have any particular schedule.

It doesn't matter how long the grief process takes, as long as you are making progress toward rebuilding your life. There are no right or wrong ways to grieve. Each person finds his own way, although we all seem to experience the same phases. We deal with them differently depending on our own personalities and dispositions.

Chapter 12

Safety at home and in your car

J.J. Bittenbinder is a security expert who worked as a Chicago police officer. He does protection videos and talk shows in which he addresses your safety. I recommend his knowledge and expertise to you. One of the things that he stresses is that you make your home a safe place.

The first thing to do is install deadbolts on your front and back doors. Trim bushes and trees away from your windows and doors so that they can be seen from the street. You can buy inexpensive timers that will turn on your lights and a radio when you are away from home. It is much nicer to return home to a house with the lights on and it's much safer, too. Motion lights on the front and rear of your home are a wonderful addition. Of course, the darn things come on if a dog or cat walks by, but they are still a good idea.

I'm not telling you these things in order to frighten you, but it is important that you make your environment a safe place to be. The same control that you've been using for the grief process should now be used to make your "personal space" safe and secure.

If you are a person who enjoys pets, a nice big dog would be a good idea. Any breed will do. It can be a German shepherd, Rottweiler, Doberman or a Heinz 57 mutt. There is something so comforting about a friendly bark and a wet kiss from your canine friend when you return home. I have a little terrier. My kids call him "the cockroach". He looks a lot like Stripe in the movie, "*Gremlins*". He probably isn't the brightest dog God ever put on this earth, but he barks like a dog possessed when any stranger approaches the house, and that makes him worth a million dollars to me.

Buying a cellular phone is a good idea too. I carry mine with me everywhere. It fits neatly into my purse. I have never had to use it to call for help but it is a wonderful piece of insurance.

I commute 20 miles one way to work and I work swing shift, which means that I get home around 11:30 p.m. Part of the road that I drive goes by a dam and is pretty deserted at that time of night. One night I got a flat tire. I pulled the car over to the side of the road and took a long look. It was flatter than a pancake. No problem, I thought, I know how to change a tire. I got the jack out of the trunk and noticed that it was a fancy little number that Tony had bought. It had some kind of hydraulic gizmo to lift the car. I got the thing into position and started to lift the car. The thing froze and there was the car with one wheel completely off the ground. The jack wouldn't work at all and the car wouldn't go up or down. I was 8 miles away from town. No help for it, I had to start walking. Scary? You bet.

I walked about an eighth of a mile when a pickup truck pulled over in front of me and offered me a ride. A million thoughts played tag in my mind. I offered up a silent plea to my knees. "Please knees, don't fail me now. Left foot, right foot". The truck driver turned out to be a good Samaritan, but it could easily have been a very dangerous situation. The very next day I bought the cellular phone and I haven't gone anywhere without it since that time. I consider the monthly service charge to be very inexpensive insurance.

I believe that you can buy a cellular phone almost anywhere and can even get ones that are programmed to call AAA or the police by simply pushing one button. I recommend this little bit of security to you. Mine has certainly given me a sense of safety, no matter where I am.

By burglar-proofing your home, having a dog as an early warning system, and calling 911 immediately, you have tilted the odds in your favor. Most burglars don't want to be the center of attention and will run away if you have taken all the proper precautions and are making a lot of noise - burglar alarm etc. is not a bad idea. Most importantly, don't be afraid, be prepared. You have grown and changed so much during your rookie year. This is just one more challenge and you're equal to it.

Chapter 13

Beam me up Scotty!

After I had been widowed for about 10 months, I was convinced that I should be feeling better and couldn't understand why I still cried at the drop of a hat. I was a 44-year-old woman with two children who had always been reasonably normal and suddenly everything was a challenge. I noticed one evening on my way home from work that my shoulders noticeably relaxed when I turned onto my little street. I hadn't realized that I was so tense until that moment.

I got out an old address book and thought seriously about calling people I hadn't seen or heard from in years. Somehow the past seemed much more comfortable than the present. The good old days seemed golden, warm and loving to me and I wanted to return to the past. It is amazing how the mind will discard all the unpleasantness from the past and leave you with such lovely memories - lovely but not necessarily accurate!

I even thought about calling a boy I had been engaged to before I met Tony. Luckily, sanity returned in time to spare me from calling a middle aged man who probably has 4.1 children, a wife who would not understand, a dog, 2 cats, a mortgage and a belly that would make W.C. Fields proud. Thank you to my brain for kicking in and sparing me from that embarrassment.

Most of the widows and widowers that I deal with in my line of work are newly widowed, although there are many I have met who are in the middle stages of the grieving process.

I remember being dispatched to one woman's home because she was having a problem with "funny phone calls". She was somewhere in her 60s, and looked like a typical grandma - gray hair pulled back into a bun, eyes that looked right into mine, lines on her face that showed that she had seen a few winters. She had a lovely smile, which she showed often even though she was frightened by the phone calls from a garden variety, heavy breather.

During the course of the conversation she told me that she had been widowed, twice! I couldn't believe it. I asked her how she had coped with this grief not once but twice. I'll never forget her reply. "One day at a time, honey." I asked her if it had gotten easier and she said that it wasn't easier, just different. The first time everything was new and awful. By the time she lost her second husband she knew what to expect.

I asked her if she thought about getting married again and her answer makes me laugh to this day. She looked straight into my eyes and said, "No way honey, this time I'll just sleep with 'em."

It is funny how perceptions change during this period of time. It is almost like being a teenager again. One day everything is too wonderful to be true, and the next day is awful.

I was driving home from work one day after Tony had been gone for almost a year and I noticed a yellow house. There were children's toys outside in the backyard. The screen door was standing open and the whole place seemed warm and inviting. I could almost smell the aroma of freshly baked cookies. The longing for that happy time in my life when my kids were little and my husband was alive became so strong that I had to pull the car over to the side of the road and have a good cry.

About a month later, I noticed the yellow house again. The screen door was still standing open - actually, it was hanging off one hinge, the yellow paint was peeling, the weeds were at least 3 feet tall, and one of the widows was broken. The toys were in the same place and I noticed they appeared to be rusted. To paraphrase Bette Davis, "What a dump." I pulled the car over to the side of the road again. This time, I couldn't drive until I stopped laughing.

This period of time is one of change and transition. I remember it clearly as being a time when I would have liked to have been anywhere but where I was. Even the French Foreign Legion had a certain appeal. Sometimes it seemed that I was like a long-tailed cat in a room full of rockers. I didn't know which way to jump.

You will probably feel a lot of the same things that I felt, things that every widow or widower feels in one way or another. Not to worry, these emotions are perfectly normal.

It was during this period of transition that I realized that I would have to change jobs in order to earn more money. I was still working for a retail store and was not making enough to support myself. I answered an ad for a dispatcher at Pleasant Valley.

I'll never forget that interview as long as I live. It went well simply because I was on auto-pilot. They called me back for a second interview and I was hired. I had some previous experience as a police dispatcher and that was what they were looking for. To say that I was scared would be the understatement of the century. Nevertheless, I gathered what little courage I had left and started to work.

Looking back now from the safe vantage point of 8 years on the job, 6 years as an officer, I would have to say it was one of the smartest things I have ever done. But it didn't feel too wonderful at the time. Some of the things that happened on the job are really funny and make me laugh to this day.

One story in particular stands out in my mind. A lady had fallen in her apartment and was unable to get up. Two units were dispatched. The other officer got there first and picked the lady up and helped her to her chair. When I got there I was annoyed and concerned because the officer who got there first hadn't checked her carefully for injuries, before he helped her up. He was new to the job and wasn't aware of the protocol regarding a careful check before touching anyone who has fallen.

The lady was in her 90's and not very verbal. She kept muttering something about hurt. I reached over to check her hips to make sure she hadn't broken one of them. Her hip seemed soft and spongy to me. I couldn't understand it and wondered if they were some soft tissue damage. My thoughts were whirling. What a screw up if she had been moved with a broken hip. I squeezed her hip again and it was really soft and really spongy. Oh dear. She was making little protest sounds.

I lifted her shirt so that I could see if there was any bruising. Oh no! The hip that I had been squeezing was really her breast, which time and gravity had moved to the area of her hipbone.

To say that I was embarrassed would be an understatement. I didn't know what to do or say, so I stroked her head and told her she was going to be fine, there was no damage that I could see. Well, wouldn't you know it? Her wig fell off and landed on the floor. I quickly picked it up and put it back on her head. Unfortunately, it was backwards and the little curls were hanging down in front of her eyes.

I glanced over my shoulder at the rookie officer and all I could see were his back and shoulders shaking. He was laughing so hard he was hanging on to the wall to keep from falling down. I muttered something to my poor victim about not hesitating to call us again if she ever needed help. Then I slunk out the door.

To this day when the officers are sitting around telling war stories, that is one of their favorites. You can hear them whooping with laughter a block away.

It is all part of the rebuilding process. You are progressing and you are progressing beautifully. I know it's tough, but nothing worthwhile is ever easy.

Chapter 14

Loneliness Part 1

During the first couple of years, loneliness is one of the worst emotions for a widow or a widower. I can remember being lonely with people all around me. When my son graduated from high school and from college, his father's absence was more painful than usual and the loneliness became even more intense. On some occasions it would feel like a lump in my throat or my chest. I know that those of you who are reading this know what I'm talking about. It's a miserable feeling.

I've always enjoyed reading, especially history. I decided to search for figures in history who dealt with widowhood and went on to live their lives, some with great success.

■■■

President Andrew Jackson was president from 1829 to 1837. His wife, Rachel Robards Jackson, was with him every step of the way. Their marriage was a controversial one because Rachel had been married previously and there was some question about whether or not her divorce was final before their marriage. When married, the scandal followed them.

Rachel Jackson died shortly before he was sworn in as the seventh President of the United States. He was 52 years old when his wife died.

He hung a portrait of his wife on the wall opposite his bed so "she'll be the first face I see in the morning."

He served two terms as president after his wife died. According to history he was a man of the people, a two-fisted brawler and a hero of the War of 1812. "Old Hickory" challenged someone who had slandered his wife to a duel. He was criticized for his uncivilized behavior, to which he replied, "I'm just sorry I didn't shoot one and hang the other."

His great love for his wife was the stuff of legends. He died June 8, 1845, and he was buried beside his Rachel at the Hermitage near Nashville, Tennessee.

* *

Mary Todd Lincoln married Abraham Lincoln in 1842. According to history, theirs was a stormy marriage. President Lincoln was assassinated on April 15, 1865.

During the years after her husband's death, Mrs. Lincoln quarreled with everyone around her and became manic in her spending habits. Her son, Robert, had her committed to a private sanitarium in 1875 for about a year. She was declared to be sane in 1876. How much of her bizarre behavior was grief and how much was her normal personality is anybody's guess.

Mrs. Lincoln had much more to deal with than most. Three of her four sons predeceased her and she had been treated badly during the Civil War, actually accused of being, at worst, a Southern spy or, at least a Southern sympathizer.

There doesn't seem to be any doubt that she loved her husband deeply and was unable to cope with being along. Her wedding ring was engraved "Love is Eternal."

She lived for 16 years after the assassination of her husband. History doesn't record her doing anything much other than grieving. She died on July 16, 1882, at the home of a married sister, and was buried beside Abraham Lincoln in the Lincoln Tomb outside Springfield, Illinois.

■■■

Alexandrina Victoria was Queen of England from 1837 to 1901. She married her cousin, Albert, Prince of Saxe-Coborg-Gotha, in 1840. Theirs was a marriage of state that grew into a love match. They produced 9 children, most of whom married into the royal houses of Europe. Prince Albert died in 1861 and Queen Victoria went into an extended period of mourning that some historians feel lasted for the rest of her life.

She enjoyed great popularity with her people, especially during the last twenty years of her reign. Her Golden Jubilee in 1887 and her Diamond Jubilee in 1897 were occasions of great rejoicing in Great Britain. She reigned for 63 years, 40 of those years after Prince Albert died.

During her reign after Prince Albert's death, she worked with many prime ministers. Only one had her confidence, Benjamin Disraeli, who secured for the Queen the title of Empress of India in 1876.

The many years of her reign were marked by her devotion to duty, honesty, concern regarding family life, and patriotism. Her reign showed a marked rise in the fortunes of the middle class. Most of her remarkable accomplishments followed the death of Prince Albert.

■■■

No chapter on widows and widowers would be complete without mentioning the Kennedy widows, Ethel and Jacqueline. Both were terrific examples of extremely strong women who faced the pain of widowhood in the glare of the spotlight.

Jacqueline went on to raise her children, marry again, be widowed again and finally to return to New York where she enjoyed her life as a devoted mother and grandmother. She was a patron of the arts and was involved as an editor for a major publisher.

She epitomized for many, grace under pressure, and I must admit that her example of control during her husband's state funeral influenced me. She stood at the foot of the stairs at the church and who can forget the picture of this magnificent woman with her children beside her or her 3-year-old son saluting the casket that carried his father? She led the nation in dignified grief at a time when her own heart must have been broken. What courage.

I've always thought that Ethel Kennedy was forgotten because she lived in the shadow of her sister-in-law. She too epitomized courage to me. Pregnant with her eleventh child, she rode the train with her husband's body on board in order to let the country grieve with her.

She has since gone on to finish raising her children and is very active in charity events like the Special Olympics. Her great skill at parenting is evident in the success of her children. Some are in public service, while others are involved in many forms of charity work. She too, is a classic example of grace under pressure.

Both women were examples to the rest of the world.

* *

There have been so many widows and widowers before us, and there will be so many after us. We are all threads that make up the fabric of life. It encouraged me tremendously to realize that I am one of many and not alone. You, too, are not alone.

Chapter 15

Loneliness Part 2

It took me a long time to understand that people who tried to help were really operating from a mindset that wanted me to "get over it." There were a few others who felt that I should probably grieve for the rest of my life and turn my home and my life into a shrine. It seemed that they liked the idea of my spending my nights wandering through the hills wearing a long black veil, mourning for my lost love. Very dramatic, but not very practical.

I have compiled my own top 10 list of suggestions that I received for coping during the first couple of years after Tony died.

1. Eat something, you'll feel better.
2. Take a trip, you need a change of scene.
3. Concentrate on the children, they're your job now.
4. Sell the house and buy something smaller.
5. Get a new hairdo and go to the theater.
6. Get a new hobby, bird watching is good.
7. Don't think about it.
8. Clean out the house and get rid of all of Tony's things.
9. You need a good man in your bed and I volunteer (spoken by a classic leech type).
10. Start dating, there is a really attractive man just up the block.

During the first year or so my sense of humor was not operating at full capacity and I didn't find a lot to laugh about, especially with regard to these various suggestions and many others. Now, I look back and some of the things on the list seem so funny to me. Number 9 is my favorite. What a jerk he was! I am not actively grieving now, but he is still a jerk! Yes, there is justice.

During the first two years, fighting the loneliness became my number 1 priority. I was worried about the effect it was having on my health and about the effect the tremendous sadness was having on my children.

It was during this period of time that I started walking every day. I would walk during my lunch hour at work. I started with just one block up and back. After about 4 months I was up to 2 miles. During my walks there were no phones, no interruptions, and I was able to think about my situation and about what I wanted for myself and my children. Sometimes I would go over the events of the past couple of years and try to make sense out of everything that had happened. Walking worked for me and helped me a lot. I still had a lot of issues to be resolved and a lot of grief to work through, but because of the walking, I was sleeping better and was in much better condition to face and deal with whatever life threw at me.

It was also during this period that I started writing - letters to family, a family history, a paper that chronicled the events surrounding Tony's death and my feelings during that time. Writing was a real catharsis for me. Once I put it on paper and read and reread it, I could clearly understand all of the events that had swirled around me.

I was very fortunate because at that time the chief of Public Safety offered me the chance to leave the dispatch desk and join the officers out in the field. I would be the third woman in the 30-year history of Pleasant Valley Public Safety Department. He gave me a couple of days to think about it. I did lots of walking, thinking, analyzing, and just plain old worrying about the decision. I finally decided "What the heck, Columbus took a chance." Of course, he got lost.

My first day on the job gave me a pretty good idea of what I was in for. An elderly gentleman had listed his home for sale. The real estate saleswoman had picked up a client and arrived at the home. She pulled out a key, put it in the front door and announced, "As we enter, you will see the marble foyer with a view into the living room." She threw open the door and extended her arm for the client to enter first. There on the floor was the home owner. He had died sometime during the night. The saleswoman screamed. The client screamed. The neighbors heard the commotion and called us. That was my first day on the job.

After calming the saleswoman and her client, my training officer and I took charge of the scene, and notified all the proper agencies, then stood by to make sure the scene was not disturbed. I had plenty of second thoughts about my career decision as we waited for the coroner. I realized as we waited there that death is not always the enemy. In this gentleman's case, death was a welcomed friend. He was in his 90s and his health was failing. Death was a relief for him and a revelation for me. I started looking at the whole thing in a different light.

One of the most important things that you can do to help ease the loneliness is to take an active and aggressive role in fighting it. For instance, if you're alone and the loneliness seems unbearable, go out somewhere. It doesn't matter much where - to the store, to a friend's house, to the local mall or the nursery to buy a rosebush for planting. Return home and plant the bush. The whole purpose behind this is to take control and change your focus. The loneliness will probably still be with you, but you are doing something positive to help yourself and that alone will help you to feel better about yourself and your situation.

Starting a project of some kind can be pretty helpful, too. One of the things that I did to change my focus was to weed the bank opposite my house and replant the whole bank with roses and wildflowers. I live on a dead end street and the field opposite me was covered with weeds that the owner would spray a couple of times a year. The whole project took me a couple of months of working a few hours a day. Now it is simply a maintenance project and it looks wonderful. It is amazing how good it felt to rip those weeds out of the soil. I'm sure the psychologists and psychiatrists would see something Freudian in those feelings, but what the heck? It worked.

During the first two years or so of widowhood, I did a lot of thinking about my place in the world. Somewhere along the line I realized that I am a link in the chain of life. No more, no less. It's very comforting to me to realize that I am not the first widow and I won't be the last. I do my best and that is really all I can ask of myself.

It also helped me to seek out the company of other widows and widowers. Talking to them really helped a lot. One lady in particular, Barbara, worked at the store where I worked when Tony died. I told her a lot of the things that I was feeling during those first awful months and Barbara, God bless her, would say, "oh, that's perfectly normal, I felt those things and so did Sue, Jack and Bobbie." Sometimes she would make suggestions about things to try to help with the ongoing grieving process. Sometimes they worked, sometimes not, but it helped to have that feedback.

Chapter 16

Decisions - Decisions - Decisions

There will be a lot of decisions to make. Some important, some not so important. These will be your decisions to make and you will probably receive a lot of unsolicited advice - that includes this book as well as any other book on grieving. You can give the advice whatever degree of importance you feel it deserves. Some suggestions should be dismissed out of hand, while others are good and should be used to your advantage.

1. *What to do about your wedding ring. Do you wear it or not?* This question, along with many others, will depend on your comfort level. Do whatever makes you the most comfortable. Some widows move the ring to their right hand. Some continue wearing it on their wedding finger. I put my ring along with Tony's in a ring box and put them away in a trunk along with all the cards, letters, funeral notices, memorial cards and the eulogy that I wrote for Tony. I intend for my kids to have these things when I am gone and they can do whatever they want to with them. At first I felt naked without the ring that I had worn for so long, but I adjusted to it after a while.

2. *How to handle the nosyheimers who ask questions that hurt or embarrass you.* This is a tough one. I guess handling it on a nosy question by nosy question basis would be best. I remember when I was in the grocery store several months after Tony's death. A man named Jerry, who was married to a coworker of mine and who I knew casually, waved to

me and walked over to where I was standing. He expressed his sympathy and asked how I was doing. We talked for a minute or two and then he sidled over close to me and in an undertone asked, "Are you gonna get to keep the house?" A thousand replies whirled through my mind. For instance, "No, I'm taking up residence at the poor farm first thing in the morning," or "Yes, but I had to take a second job. You can find me any night out on 25th and Mac Donald plying my trade," or "No, but my friends are taking up a collection for me. Have you got 50,000 dollars you can spare?" or "Yes, but I had to rent rooms out to the local degenerates in order to make ends meet. Care to move in?" You will be happy to know that I took the high road and answered the question, changed the subject, and left without letting him know what a clod I thought he was. Amazing control!

3. *What to do with personal belongings and clothing.* This one is easy. Do whatever you want to do with these things - charity, storage or giving them to friends or relatives. Keep whatever you want to keep without paying any attention to what anyone else suggests. To this day I have a jacket of Tony's that I wear whenever I need a little extra courage. These are now your things and you can dispose of them in any way you see fit.

4. *What is my status with my in-laws?* This one is easy, too. Your status should be whatever you want it to be. If you want to continue a close relationship with them, do so. If not, distance yourself from them, if you can without hurting them. After all, they have suffered a loss too. My husband's father became, my father, when Tony died. It continues that way to this day. I told Dad once that Tony left me with two terrific kids and a set of parents. Pretty nice legacy.

5. *How should I live the rest of my life?* Ah, yes. This decision is the biggie. As with all the other decisions you will be making for yourself, this one is yours and yours alone. I think the best answer was given to me by the widow in Pleasant Valley when she said, "One day at a time, honey."

Chapter 17

Hey, where did everybody go?

One of the hardest things for me to deal with in the first couple of years following Tony's death was the change in my social life. It took a while to sink in that I was no longer part of a couple. Most of my friends were married and still doing the married social thing.

For the first year, I didn't go anywhere I didn't absolutely have to go. I remember that as being a terrible time. I would go to the market, to my job, to family get-togethers that I couldn't dodge, and occasionally out with friends for a quiet dinner. I remember my hairdresser telling me about the customs in her homeland. She told me that in Taiwan a widow was expected to retreat to her family's home for a period of 2 years. During that time she would not leave the house and it was a time of enforced grieving. At the end of the 2-year grief period, she would emerge from the home and pick up her life again. Sounded pretty grim to me.

I felt the most comfortable at home with my children. My daughter, Tammy, was dating her future husband at the time. One day the two of them came to me and told me they wanted to get married. I approved wholeheartedly although I had mixed emotions. I was delighted for Tammy and Mark, but kind of sad for me. I hadn't realized until that time how much I depended on Tammy to be there, listen to me, and be my friend. It must have been very hard for Tammy. She lost her father and saw her mother turn into this grieving person she hardly knew. I overheard Tammy tell Mark that he didn't know what fear was. She did. It was "watching my strong mother crumble." Tammy never complained about the double duty she was doing, but their impending marriage was a wake-up call for me. It was time to pick up the threads of my life again.

This was a difficult time for me. I wasn't sure where I belonged in the social scheme of things and realized quickly that I had very little in common with my married friends. They were still my dear friends, but suddenly it was as though we spoke a different language. I can remember thinking "What the heck is going on here?" We used to talk and laugh for hours and suddenly I couldn't think of anything to say. What was worse was that I didn't give a hoot about problems in suburbia! I felt like the odd man out and wasn't sure what, if anything, I could do about the problem.

One girlfriend of mine, Carol, came over to my house one day. She seemed really nervous and upset. I got her a cup of coffee and sat down with her to listen to what I thought would be some kind of problem that she was having. She looked down at her hands and said, "Diane, I hope you'll forgive me and understand, but I can't be around you anymore. The sadness in your eyes is more than I can stand." She hugged me and left. I tried to understand, really tried. I think I do understand. It is sad, but I know that being around me at that time was just too much for Carol. I'm not a psychologist, but I imagine being around me reinforced the fact that we are all mortal. When Tony died, my friends realized again that we are all going to die, and that is a scary thought.

My friend Norma, with the panda purse, told me that she didn't feel comfortable in my home anymore because she could see Tony everywhere. I really understood, perhaps more than I understood Carol's reaction. Norma grieved deeply for Tony, and in her own way, for me too. She felt that I would never be the same and she missed both Tony and me.

These two little episodes are not uncommon for widows and widowers according to what I have heard. One gentleman in Pleasant Valley was not so understanding.

I was dispatched to a home to check on the welfare of the man who lived there. He had mentioned to his daughter on the phone that his life was over and all he needed to do was end it. I knocked on the door and he invited me in and had me sit down. The sadness on his face was like a cloud around him. He kept clenching and unclenching his fists. He told me that a couple of the fellows in his golf group had suggested that he start attending social functions again and perhaps take a lady or two out to dinner after the golf game. He was furious, heartbroken, and felt completely cut off from everyone and everything. We talked for over an hour.

He was so angry that his friends would even suggest that he see another woman. He felt that these people were being disrespectful to the memory of his late wife. His overwhelming desire at that time was to find his friends, punch them in the nose, then end his life. He talked and talked and talked. Most of the things he was upset about were just superfluous things. He was really upset because his wife had died and he didn't know what to do next.

I called for the nurse to respond to my location and when she got there I was delighted to see that it was Ellie Wynn. Ellie had also been widowed. She had some wonderful suggestions for this man, and he listened because we made him aware that we were both widows and knew what he was feeling.

By the time we left, any danger of this man doing harm to himself or his friends seemed to have vanished. All he really needed was for someone to listen to him. We listened.

I saw him again about a year later. He was locked out and I responded to open his door. At first I didn't recognize him. There was a smile on his face and he even made a joke about having locked himself out. He said he was in a hurry because he was late for a golf date and after the golf game he was to meet a group of friends for dinner. Good for him!

What to do? Where to go? How to start living my life again? All were questions to which I had no answers. I still talked to my girlfriends on the phone and still would occasionally join my friends for a dinner out, but time spent with married couples was uncomfortable for me.

A friend of mine by the name of Tom Calkins was between marriages at this time. Tom was the kind of guy who always seemed to be between marriages. He would serve as my escort to various social things, and it was the best of all possible worlds for me. There were absolutely no romantic overtones because Tom was a brother-type buddy. Going out again helped me tremendously. The gap between actively grieving and the world as I had known was like a chasm of the Grand Canyon.

Tom was witty, charming and kind. He friendship meant a lot to me at that time and helped me reenter the social world. Not the world of couples, exactly, but the world of movies, dinners out, and parties where the hostess has planned for an even number of guests.

Spending time with Tom during this period of my rookie year helped me to focus on others outside my world of grief and worry. Tom was the kind of fellow who always had a crisis of one kind or another. They were always funny to me and I enjoyed watching Tom try to wriggle out of one scrape or another. For instance, one Thanksgiving he had scheduled two dates, one for a noon luncheon and the other for an elegant dinner at 6. Somehow or other both of these ladies knew about the other and they were actively competing for Tom's attentions. It was really silly. I laughed and realized, not for the first time, that laughter is healing.

The kind of social planning that requires an even number of guests can really hurt a widow or widower's feelings. It is as though you are suddenly not as desirable as you were when you were the other half of a couple. I don't believe that this sort of thing is done intentionally. People who have not been widowed do not understand how little things can seem so huge and so hurtful to a person who has been widowed.

Chapter 18

The rookie year is over. So why don't I feel better?

It was a really nasty surprise to me to find that after making so many adjustments during the first year of widowhood, I didn't feel too much better when the second year started. The roller coaster started back down again and it took a lot of work on my part to get back to level track.

My friend, Diane Steinberg, said much the same thing to me not too long ago. Somehow we expect the second year to be so much easier. Baloney! It isn't. It is just tough in a different way. The shock has worn off and you are left with the cold, hard facts. It is a good idea to take a good hard look at your life now and decide whether you need to make changes in some areas or not. If you do, go ahead after careful thought and make those changes.

A good idea would be to write down on a piece of paper the positives and the negatives in your life. The fact that you have been widowed would have to be # 1 on the negative side of the paper, but it isn't the begin-all, end-all that it seemed to be one short year ago.

The positives on your paper should reflect all the adjustments that you have made. Keep in mind that you have survived your first anniversary, first Christmas, first Thanksgiving and first everything else without your spouse. Not only that, you have survived with your mind intact. You have created a safe environment for yourself. You are taking care of your health, both mental and physical. You have done a lot of positive things this past year and you are a stronger, happier, and more understanding person than you were a year ago.

After your rookie year is over it is a good time to take small steps back into the real world which continued turning while you were grieving. I heard a song once that started out, "Why does the sun keep on shining", and it goes on and on about all the things that go on while we grieve. Take as much time as you need to reenter the world of the nongrieving. It seems like a different planet. It is scary, but you can do it. You've already proved that you are equal to any challenge.

Chapter 19

Dating
(or)
How many frogs do I have to kiss?

There will come a point when you will probably consider whether or not to date. This is an individual decision. There is no right or wrong. Some widows and widowers never date or remarry. Others do so very quickly. Others take a lot of time making up their minds about whether to date or not.

I would advise caution in this area. It was a real culture shock when I started dating again. Most of the men that I went out with were fine men and I enjoyed spending time with them. However, there were a couple of real jerks, and it shattered my self-confidence that I had been unable to spot these turkeys before I dated them.

I won't bore you with the details so I'll try to summarize my various experiences in the murky world of dating.

I dated a few gentlemen that I met without really knowing them first. That is always a crap shoot. You never know until you go out with them who or what they are. A good piece of advice here is to agree to meet a date at a restaurant or mall or somewhere else that is crowded for the first couple of dates or so. After that you will have a pretty good idea as to whether this person is one to trust or not.

I am flattered and humbled to tell you that several of these fine men proposed to me after just a few dates. I turned them down because I knew that what they were looking for was something that I wasn't, or they wanted different things from life than I wanted. Most of these gentlemen are still my friends and I keep track of them and wish them all well.

There were a couple of stinkers and I am embarrassed to admit to you that I didn't spot it right away and was fooled for quite a while. Mea culpa!

I've always been a very trusting soul as far as my personal life is concerned. I value honesty and personal integrity above almost anything else, and one man in particular was so dishonest and so arrogant in his dishonesty that I really didn't catch on until some time after we had stopped dating. At first I was hurt, but then I thought it over and I believe that I dodged a bullet without knowing there was any danger. Lucky Diane. He is someone else's problem now.

The down side of all this is that it caused me to question whether or not I understood what was going on in the world around me. I know this is a concern for you, too. Try to not give it any more importance than it deserves. Honor, honesty, dignity and a sense of humor are still important and it doesn't matter what year we're in, those are still the most important things. Don't worry too much about the frogs. Yes, they are out there, but you're smart. You'll be able to spot them without seeing the warts!

This reminds me of a story. A woman was walking down a road in the country during the winter. She saw a snake lying by the side of the road, half frozen. The snake said to her, "Beautiful lady, please pick me up and take me home. I am almost frozen and I will die if you don't help me." The lady said to the snake, "But I am worried because you are a snake." He replied, "I won't hurt you, beautiful lady. Please take me home and let me sleep by your fire." She was a kind soul so she picked the snake up, put it in her pocket, and took it home. She put it down on the hearth by the fireplace and brought it some milk to drink.

The next morning she arose and went into the living room to see how the snake had fared during the night. She picked it up and it bit her. She cried to the snake, "How could you bite me when I saved your life, brought you home, fed you and allowed you to sleep by my fire?" The snake replied, "It's your own fault. You knew I was a snake when you picked me up!"

The message is very clear. Be careful. You weren't born yesterday. You have lived a few years and you are intelligent. Use your common sense and you should be fine.

I can almost hear the question from here: "Where do I go to meet people?" Before I answer that, let me tell you where not to go. I do not recommend bars or singles clubs. From what I hear from some of my single friends, those places are meat markets and will be very hard on your ego and may even cause you to question what planet you're on. The last thing that you need at this point in your life is to be rated on a scale of 0 to 10. Avoid those places.

"Well, where then?" I hear you cry. I have a top ten list for that, too:

1. Church
2. Work
3. Friends' homes
4. Volunteer worksites
5. Supermarkets
6. Laundromats
7. Parks - national, state and local
8. Cruises
9. Tour groups
10. Benefit dinners and dances

Again, the most important thing will be to remember who is in control. You are. Use the common sense you have always used and don't let loneliness or grief dictate your decisions about dating or anything else. You will be fine.

I remember very clearly a woman that I met while responding to a call in Pleasant Valley. She approached Officer Bill Flanigan and myself as we left the home following the call. Bill Flanigan is a tall, handsome man. I'm sure she was much more interested in talking to him than to me, but I was there so I listened in. She told Bill that she was just moving into that area because she had been widowed 4 times and was getting remarried in a week's time. If a woman can be said to twitter, this one twittered. She batted her eyelashes and practically cooed as she told Bill all about it. She told Bill that she was just amazed that her husband-to-be was willing to take a chance on marrying her when she had been widowed so many times before. She said that the man in question had told her he thought he'd take his chances. At this point she giggled.

I was really impressed by her performance and Bill looked bemused. I guess there really are merry widows. She qualifies as the only one I have ever met. Before you ask, I don't know the fate of husband # 5.

That reminds me of a joke about a man who had been widowed 6 times. A reporter asked him how he had come to be widowed so many times. He replied that the first 5 wives had died from eating poisoned mushrooms.

The reporter asked what had happened to wife # 6. "She was shot," replied the man. "Shot?" asked the reporter. "How did that happen?" The man replied, "She wouldn't eat the poisoned mushrooms!"

There are several do's and don'ts for dating if you choose to date.

- DO take stock of yourself and realize that you have a lifetime track record of achievement to be proud of, because you were in a long, committed and happy marriage. A salesman would say that you are a tried-and-true product.

- DO enjoy the time spent out. Go places that you enjoy going. I know that this time can be pretty frightening and stressful, but try to relax and consider it an evening out with a friend. This person must be pretty special or you wouldn't have considered going out in the first place.

- DON'T compare him or her to your late spouse. No one could possibly measure up to that comparison. It wouldn't be fair to your date or to you. It would be like comparing apples to oranges at the supermarket. Same shape and size, but very different. Besides, it was a different time and place. When you were dating your spouse, you were a different person. Events and time change a person and whether you realize it or not, you have changed a lot during the grieving process.

- DON'T pay any attention to the nosyheimers who will try to tell you what to do and how to do it. I really believe that most people who offered me advice - lots and lots of advice - did so with the purest of motives. They did so out of love and concern for me, but they didn't understand the grieving process and didn't understand what it felt like from inside.

- DON'T do anything that makes you feel uncomfortable or anxious. You have nothing to prove.

If you have gone out with someone who makes you uncomfortable, don't blame yourself and think that it might be your fault. Baloney! That person is probably not a good candidate for a second date. As I mentioned before, there are some real creeps out there. If you have unfortunately located one of them, don't hesitate to dump this nogoodnik immediately!

- DO take your time and pick your places to go. This can be an enjoyable part of your life.

- DON'T waste one second of time feeling guilty or disloyal to your late spouse. Most of the widows and widowers that I know kept all their marriage promises and proved themselves to be loyal and devoted husbands and wives. I can't speak for anyone else, but I know that Tony would be the first one to urge me to go out and enjoy myself. He'd be a one-man rooting section if he could. Real love is not selfish and your late spouse would not want you to be alone and lonely. Again, you kept all your promises when your spouse was alive - you have nothing to feel guilty or ashamed about now.

- DO go out as often or a little as you wish. Do not feel pressured to marry again or not marry again. You are the only judge of what will be best for you. Some widows and widowers make the mistake of feeling that everything will be fine if they just get remarried. Ain't necessarily so! You will be the only and final judge of this matter. Don't date "in the future." By that, I mean go out and enjoy the evening and the company without borrowing trouble from the future. Just enjoy the present and worry about the future when it gets here. The older I get, the faster it seems to get here, too.

Chapter 20

For Ladies Only

Okay girls, here is the straight skinny. There are disreputable car salesmen, appliance repair people, car repair people, and salespeople in some stores. They can probably spot you a mile away. I am not saying that they are all crooks but there are some who will take advantage of you. Again, you weren't born yesterday. Protect yourself. Take a male friend with you when you enter one of these establishments. Do your homework before you buy a new car or new anything else. Check the Blue Book for car values or ask your friends. Also, you might want to read publications that rate various products for reliability and price. You might want to check with the Better Business Bureau, Consumer Reports or government periodicals rating various products.

If you have decided that you want to sell your home and move to a smaller place or just a different place, be very careful and make sure you get independent estimates from appraisers. Do not accept just one appraisal from the real estate people. They are not in the real estate business because they are frustrated Mother Theresas, they are in the business to make money. Make sure you protect yourself. That is not to say that they will cheat you, but it is up to you to make sure of the actual value of your property.

Make certain that you have a pretty good idea what something should cost before you actually go in to purchase it. If this is a repair project, get an estimate in writing and check to make sure it is reasonable before you give the go-ahead. I know, I know, this sort of thing is sexist and shouldn't be happening, but it is a fact of life. Later, much later, you can deal with the social ramifications of this kind of behavior and lobby for some changes in the way these characters do business, but for right now you need to take care of yourself and your pocketbook. Don't be shy, you speak right up for yourself.

I know that this will be difficult for you. It was hard for me, too. We were all raised to be "good girls." We weren't supposed to make noise or cause a scene or do anything else that could be considered "unladylike." Baloney! The most important thing now is for you to protect your assets, and therefore your security. I guess one of the problems with this kind of thinking is that we all expect a knight to come along on a white horse and save us. I hate to tell you this, but don't hold your breath while waiting for him to show up. You could turn blue and you may not look good in blue!

I've never believed in the women's liberation movement. I always thought I was liberated to start with and never had time to get involved in a political movement of any kind. However, life has taught me that it is not only okay to stand up for yourself, it is mandatory. You can do this. I know you can!

One other thing before I end this chapter - you may feel as many other widows do that because your married life is over you don't have to go to the doctor and have those embarrassing tests. You know what I mean. Pap tests, breast exams and mammograms. Yes, you do have to have them. I'm sorry, but you don't get to stop doing these things. They are important to your health and therefore necessary.

Just say "yech" and get on the phone and make those appointments. As uncomfortable as these things are, after what you have survived, "they ain't nothing."

As the TV detective, *Colombo*, would say, "One more thing." If you are dating and you are in a relationship that may end up in the bedroom, CONDOMS. Yes, I said the C word. This is literally a matter of life and death. Protect yourself. I had never even heard of some of the diseases that are now present, but these diseases are a fact of life. Do not put yourself in a position of risk. Use condoms.

Chapter 21

For Men Only

I know that your wife probably made all the medical appointments for you and now that you are alone and responsible for yourself, you have put them off. It is time, past time, to call and make the appointment for the tests that are necessary for your well-being. You know which tests I'm referring to in this paragraph. Yep, the old "bend over and cough," plus all the other procedures that you know so well.

The transitions that you are experiencing now will be so much easier if you don't have health worries. You need to do the same thing that I advised the ladies to do, say "yech," pick up the phone, and call for your appointment.

It has been my experience that some men feel tremendous pain from imaginary disloyalty to their late wives. Your wife, this wonderful woman who you miss so terribly, would not want you to be alone. Your welfare was probably her main concern while she was here. If she could, she would probably urge you to enjoy your life, and if that means female companionship, that's okay too. Don't waste precious time agonizing over feeling that you are somehow "cheating" on her. This is nonsense and your wife would probably be the first one to tell you so.

The men that I have met through my job - those that I have tried to comfort and those who I have heard about too late to comfort - all shared one thing in common, a deep love and loyalty to their deceased wives. All of them suffered terribly from grief and the idea that somehow it wasn't manly to share their feelings with others. Baloney! You need to talk about these feelings as much as your female counterparts. Maybe even more.

Now, fellas I can almost hear you saying, "What can she know about what a man feels or about how it would offend my dignity to cry in front of anybody?" I agree with you. I don't know how it would feel from a man's point of view. What I do know - and I know this from years of experience on the job - your grief is every bit as real as a woman's and you too need to be able to vent your feelings. Try not to be too concerned with your dignity at this point. More simply put, the hell with it. Do whatever you need to do in order to take back control and ease some of the tension you are feeling. If this means crying in front of someone and being embarrassed about it later, so be it. The benefits far outweigh the negatives. You will be able to put your dignity coat back on later when you feel stronger and don't need to vent the way you do now.

Several months ago I was sent out on a neighborhood dispute. I spoke to one of the neighbors in an effort to mediate this dispute and resolve it in a peaceful way. The man said to me, "Diane, you don't remember me, do you? You comforted me shortly after my wife died." His eyes filled with tears while he talked about it. I honestly didn't remember because I have gone on hundreds of calls in my years with Public Safety. He noticed the blank look on my face and said, "You hugged me and whispered to me, 'It's okay to cry.' I've never forgotten it and I have cried. It helped. Thank you."

If I could I would hug every one of you who are reading this book and say to you, "It is okay to cry!"

I know you probably sneaked a peek at the "For Women Only" chapter, so you know what I am going to tell you next. I'll say it again anyway. If you do decide to date and you find yourself in a romantic situation, USE CONDOMS. In today's world this is not an unreasonable or outrageous statement. It is mandatory that you protect yourself.

Chapter 22

The Evil Twins - Guilt and Regret

Lorraine loved her husband and her children with every fiber of her being. She was a loving wife and mother. She and her husband Jim raised their children to adulthood and both were community-oriented people who were active in various worthwhile charities.

After they had been married for about 30 years, Jim's health started to fail. He had a heart condition and gradually his personality changed. He changed from a loving husband to an abusive one. The last year or so of his life he was often verbally abusive to Lorraine and sometimes even struck her. Their wonderful life together deteriorated into a nightmare of illness and abuse.

Lorraine couldn't understand what was happening, and Jim probably couldn't either. She hung in there even though she talked to friends about leaving him. Their fights became the talk of the neighborhood and on one or two occasions the police were called. The worst part of this situation lasted for about four months, and then Jim suffered a massive heart attack and died.

After the funeral and the immediate grieving period, Lorraine talked to the doctors about Jim's behavior and they told her that in all probability it was a result of his illness. His personality change was not uncommon for someone in the final stages of heart disease. Now, not only did Lorraine have to deal with grief, she had to deal with her guilt and regret regarding some of the things she had said to Jim.

She sold her home and moved closer to one of her daughters. Her life became a nightmare of regret and guilt. She did not search out help from anyone. Her grief, regret and guilt became her only companions. I am sorry to tell you that the last news I heard of Lorraine was that she was drinking heavily and rarely leaves her house.

What a tragedy. Two people died from that heart condition. Lorraine is still alive physically, but her spirit is dead.

What could she have done to help herself? As you already know, there are many avenues open for getting help. Professional help would have been a good idea at the beginning so Lorraine could rid herself of guilt and regret. Unfortunately, Lorraine was unable to face the pain of talking about what had happened to "strangers." Her family was as confused as she was by what had happened and were dealing with their own grief and loss.

No matter what the condition of your marriage, you must let go of the evil twins. It doesn't really matter if there were harsh words between you and your spouse. So what? Who would understand better than your life partner? There are no perfect marriages. If someone says that they never had an argument with their spouse, they are probably living in the most wonderful fantasy world or they are legally dead, from the neck up. Ridding yourself of this guilt is probably one of the most important things you can do at this time. Let it go. You and your spouse had arguments? Welcome to the real world. Everyone does. Let it go and forget about the words you said that you regret. Your spouse would be the first one to say, "It's okay, I'm sorry too."

The other evil twin, regret, is just as destructive to you as you rebuild your life. There is not a single person in the world who doesn't have some regret - maybe places you didn't go, things you didn't accomplish, or things left unsaid.

I wrote a long letter about two years after Tony died. In the letter I detailed all my regrets, all the things I wish that I had said but didn't and the things that I did say that I wish I could take back. I wrote about my regret for not having been more aware of Tony's medical condition and I wrote about not having intervened with the dying process that I didn't recognize at the time. Well, heck, if I'd known I would have tried to call out the Marines to stop it. When I finally finished, I read it over several times, dealt with the feelings, and finally burned it in the fireplace. Doing this helped me to let go of the evil twins. Writing or verbalizing these negative feelings and emotions is an important step during the grieving process. I recommend it to you.

The other thing that I did happened quite by accident. On my 30th wedding anniversary I went to Tony's grave. It was the first time that I had been there since the headstone was put up. I saw the words "Anthony Laird Bullock May 26,1941 - November 29, 1986," carved in the stone. When I read it my knees buckled, and I felt as though someone had punched me in the stomach. I found myself on the ground in front of his grave. I sat there for over an hour, just talking to my Tony, and telling him everything that was on my mind. The tears flowed freely and I didn't give a hoot who saw me.

Later, as I was driving home I realized that I felt lighter, calmer, and happier than I had felt in a while. It is incredible what venting can do for your soul.

If it sounds as though getting through the pain of being widowed is a lot of work, it is. It is a lot like any other project in your life - planning a course of action, setting goals, and carrying through with them are all a part of the recovery process. You can do this! Take a good look at how far you've come from a year ago. Amazing, isn't it?

Chapter 23

To Join or not to Join, that is the question.

There are many good groups that you can join if you want the fellowship of other widowers and widows. Two that come to mind are *Parents Without Partners* and *Widows Network*. There are dozens of others. If you are interested and feel that joining a group would be beneficial to you, check your local telephone book for names and addresses.

There are things you should consider before you call. Your personality is the most important thing to think about. If you are shy and have never been a joiner before, exercise caution. Look before you leap. If, however, you are very outgoing and have belonged to various clubs, this is probably right up your alley and can be invaluable in your recovery.

I attended one meeting of Widow's Network. I am by nature very shy around people I don't know. This doesn't hold true on my job. I don't know why there is a difference, but I just march into any situation like I've known these people all my life when I'm in uniform and on the job. I never said shyness made any sense. I've always been shy and it takes me time to get to know people.

About 11 months after Tony died, I decided it was time to start helping myself a bit more. A widows' group seemed a wonderful idea. I called one of the groups and decided to attend a meeting the following Saturday.

I found the place, a minor miracle given my lack of sense of direction. I sat down and two beautifully dressed and coifed women approached me and introduced themselves. They were the facilitators. They explained that they would run the meeting and assist the rest of us in dealing with the issues that had brought us to the meeting.

The meeting started, and the facilitators explained that they were widowed and explained, in turn, what the group was about and how they planned to direct the conversation. To this day I don't know what happened, but I started to cry. Remember, I don't cry in a pretty way. That is an understatement. Well, I started crying, slowly at first, but very quickly building up to a crescendo of snuffling and sniffling with a runny nose, red eyes, and a voice that wouldn't work. One of the facilitators turned to me and asked me if I wanted to share my feelings with the group.

I opened my mouth and all that came out was something between a mouse's squeak and a duck's quack. I tried again - same sound, but more volume. There I was, unable to make any sound other than that really unique squeak/quack. I was fishing around in my purse for a tissue, but no luck. It got really ugly after that! Squeak/quack snuffle, snuffle, and then repeat the sequence. Time seemed to stand still while these lovely, gracious women tried their hardest to help me with suggestions like "Diane seems to be very emotional about her feelings, maybe we should discuss that for a while."

I was finally able, by waving my hand, to get them to move on to other topics. That was the longest 10 minutes of my life. Seemed more like 10 years. As the conversation moved around the room, my tears stopped.

Both of the facilitators were very gracious, and after the meeting told me that they hoped I would continue to attend. When I finally got to my car and headed home, I felt much like a paroled ex-convict who had just left San Quentin. Joining was definitely not for me.

Since that time I have met several people who belong to one group or another and enjoy the outings and the friendship of others in the group. Joining or not joining is an individual decision for each person. Don't be afraid to join. After all, most people don't do the Diane Dance - snuffle, snuffle, sniff, sniff, squeak/quack. Set to music, I might have a big selling record on my hands. Maybe in my next life!

I returned home from that meeting and spent the rest of the afternoon talking to my daughter. Tammy has always been an excellent listener and has that innate sense of when to ask questions and when to shut up and just listen. I talked and talked and talked. Tammy, God love her, listened, and I got most of the feelings off my chest. I still had a long way to go in the grieving process, but knowing that I could talk if I needed to helped more than I can say.

Chapter 24

Who am I?

Well now, look at you! You are almost to the end of the tunnel. There is more daylight now than dark and you know, really know, that you can survive this tragedy. You will survive with everything intact. Your mind, your spirit and your zest for life are all back in varying degrees. You are looking around and you are noticing the world and the people again with interest. Your eyes are starting to sparkle and there is probably a bounce in your step. Now, now, I didn't say that you are "over it." You didn't have the measles so you can't "get over it". You are changed by your experience, by your loss. It was and will always be a life-changing experience. That doesn't mean it was all negative. You have learned a lot about yourself and how you react to the most devastating situation. You've discovered strengths in yourself that you probably didn't know existed.

Most Americans over the age of 40 can tell you exactly where they were and what they were doing when President John F. Kennedy was assassinated. It was an event that none of us will ever forget. For a lot of us, it was a time of grief and disbelief. It forever changed the way we viewed the world around us. The death of your spouse will undoubtedly have the same effect on you. You will always remember the event with sadness and it has indeed changed your life. That doesn't necessarily mean that it has changed you for the worse. Actually, it probably has changed you for the better. You are now more aware of who you are and you know - and know absolutely - how you deal with the worst life has to offer.

There will be events in your life that you would love to share with your spouse and it takes adjustment to experience these events, alone. My daughter Tammy gave birth to my first granddaughter in the same hospital where she was born. I sat on a stone bench out on the roof garden, looked up at the stars, and wondered if Tony knew that we were grandparents. I remembered the look on his face when Tammy was born. The tenderness I remembered in his eyes, makes me tear up to this day. An Indian legend says that if two people look at the Evening Star, at the same time, they are together, no matter how far apart they are. I wondered if Tony was looking at the star where he was. Somehow, that made him seem closer.

What to do now? The answer to that is simple. You live your life and you live it with the knowledge that you have survived this terrible period in your life. Good for you. You are now in a position to reach out to others who are experiencing what you have lived through. If you have the chance to reach out to someone who needs your knowledge, do so. Yes indeed, lemons to lemonade.

Occasionally, the grief will return, probably when you least expect it. This is normal and nothing to be concerned about. We have an expression in my line of work; we say that when we have dealt with a situation to our satisfaction and ended it, it can sometimes come back and "bite you on the butt." Grief and loss are that way, too. Don't be too concerned about that aspect. It is perfectly normal and you can deal with it the way you have dealt with everything else during this last couple of years or so.

I will close this book with a lovely quote from Auntie Mame. She said, "Life is a banquet and most poor suckers are starving to death."

My advice to you is, enjoy the banquet.

About the Author

Diane Bullock was married for almost 24 years when her husband Tony died suddenly. Tony and Diane had two children, one of whom was still in high school when he died.

Diane started a new career with the Public Safety Department of a large retirement community with approximately 10,000 residents in the enclave. She worked her way up from dispatcher, to officer and finally to Public Safety Captain in the 12 years she has worked there.

Diane still lives in the same house in Northern California where she and Tony raised their kids. Both children are grown, educated and leading happy, productive lives. They are Diane's proudest accomplishment.

Diane finds time to indulge her love of family, animals and along with her companion of 6 years, Max, happily tramps the High Sierra every chance she gets.

Printed in the United States
15929LVS00001B/203